GRIZZLY
BEARS

Edited by Todd R. Berger
Printed in Hong Kong

97   98   99   00   01   5   4   3   2   1

Library of Congress Cataloging-in-Publication Data
Turbak, Gary.
Grizzly bears / Gary Turbak.
p.   cm. — (World life library)
Includes bibliographical references (p. 71) and index.
ISBN 0-89658-334-1
1. Grizzly bear. I. Title. II. Series.
QL737.C27T87   1997
599.74'466—dc20   96-42373
                                             CIP

Published by Voyageur Press, Inc.
123 North Second Street, P.O. Box 338, Stillwater, MN 55082 U.S.A.
612-430-2210, fax 612-430-2211

Please write or call, or stop by, for our free catalog of natural history publications. Our toll-free number to place an order or to obtain a free catalog is 800-888-WOLF (800-888-9653).

Educators, fundraisers, premium and gift buyers, publicists, and marketing managers: Looking for creative products and new sales ideas? Voyageur Press books are available at special discounts when purchased in quantities, and special editions can be created to your specifications. For details contact the marketing department.

Page one: Photo © Fred Hirschmann
Page four: Photo © Gary Schultz
Front cover: Photo © Gary Schultz
Back cover: Photo © Kennan Ward

GRIZZLY
BEARS

Gary Turbak

Voyageur Press

Contents

Introduction

Inside the earth, the great bear awakens. Muscles dormant since last fall twitch with the electricity of a new year. Biological systems that months ago slowed to a crawl start to rev again. The bruin's heartbeat picks up pace, and deep breaths come more frequently. The animal's eyes open, but in the blackness of the den there is little to see. With a low woof, the bear rolls onto its belly and shakes its massive head. Following timeless genetic instructions that it could never begin to understand, the great grizzly crawls from its den into the high-country cold of another spring.

Thus begins the age-old march through the seasons for North America's—and arguably the world's—premier carnivore. For millennia, the emerging grizzly sauntered onto a landscape it alone controlled. The bear's size, strength, and aggressive personality largely freed the bruin from fear. It was the dominant species, capable of ruling any lands it cared to colonize.

But one slender shadow lay across the grizzly's path. Humankind has always nurtured a keen interest in bears. Perhaps it is because of our shared omnivorous appetite. Or that we both walk on the soles of our feet. Or that the bear often uses its forefeet like hands. Or the female grizzly's devotion to her young. Or the bear's apparent miracle of rebirth performed each spring.

Whatever the reason, bears have long been intertwined with humanity—from cave art to Goldilocks to Teddy to Pooh to Smokey to Ursa Major in the northern sky. Some early hunting clans worshiped a grizzly god. In some societies, a necklace of bear claws granted the aboriginal wearer power and strength. And even today some cultures find healing and potency in ursine body parts.

Several years ago, in the wilds of northern Montana, an eclectic group of people—biologists, Native Americans, counter-culture free souls, the spiritual, and the simply curious—gathered for three days of ursine adulation called a bear honoring. The people were paying tribute to grizzlies and to the brother-hood of bears and humanity. The honoring included sacred fires, purifying sweats, chants at dawn, and much talk of Mother Earth, birth, death, grizzlies, and the imminent emergence of the bears from their

From a lofty perch, the grizzly surveys its vast domain. (Photo © Tom Walker)

Incredibly powerful and keenly attuned to its surroundings, the grizzly has long been the dominant creature in its environment. Humans, with their weapons and ability to alter the habitat, are the great bear's only enemies. (Photo © Robert E. Barber)

dens. In addition, there were signs of magic. A bluebird showed up weeks earlier than normal to perch at the side of a Native American medicine woman. Two inches (5 cm) of snow—required for a ceremony— fell quietly overnight. When the celebrants needed a full moon, the clouds parted to reveal one in the nighttime sky. New Age mumbo jumbo, you say? Perhaps. But it is difficult to imagine such an event structured around any other animal.

Just about everyone who cares about wildlife thinks the grizzly is something special. The grizzly is exquisitely muscled, strong almost beyond belief, rippled with furry beauty, and intensely aware of its surroundings. Striding across a mountain meadow, the grizzly presents a picture of confidence, grace, lordliness, and raw power. While most creatures simply respond to their surroundings, grizzlies seem to be in charge, to create their own destiny.

But so do humans, and therein lies the rub. When Native Americans and grizzlies first came face to face on some stretch

From cave art to fairy tales to telephoto lenses, people have always had an intense interest in grizzlies. (Photo © Curt and Cary Given)

of desolate tundra, a rare kind of interspecific standoff ensued. Grizzlies had claws and jaws, but the people had weapons. The bears exhibited tremendous physical power, but humans possessed that great equalizer: intellect. A time of peaceful coexistence resulted. People and bears remained attuned to one another, engaged in a perpetual minuet of joust and parry, fear and respect, admiration and abhorrence.

Then, a couple of centuries ago, this delicate equilibrium crumbled. Humans, equipped with gunpowder and the ability to alter the landscape on a massive scale, became the unquestioned sovereign species, and the grizzly's stock—at least in the lower 48 states of the U.S.—plummeted. Today, the great bear that once dominated North America and much of the rest of the world exists at the pleasure of mere people.

Origin, History, and Range of the Grizzly Bear

The man stood in the dim, smoky light of the cave. The day's hunt had gone well. There was meat. Now, his belly full, he turned his attention to another pursuit. Between his fingers he held a short, blunted stick. In a bowl-shaped piece of dried animal hide lay separate piles of granulated earthy pigments—red, ocher, black. He dipped the stick in the primitive paint and, perhaps reliving a hundred experiences, began to draw on the cave wall. Gradually, the full, rounded body and elongated snout of a bear flowed from the artist's mind to the stone surface. It was a big bruin, and the man glanced anxiously at the cave entrance to be sure the flesh-and-blood version did not catch him off guard. He knew that living with bears was a special proposition. What he could not know was that it would remain thus for the next 20,000 years.

The first animal to earn the ursine label (*Ursus minimus* or "little bear") appeared perhaps eight million years ago in Europe and Asia. A few million years later, *Ursus etruscus*, the progenitor of a line of large animals with short and stocky legs, thick torsos, large heads, and strong necks, emerged from the evolutionary mix. These creatures, like people, walked primarily on the soles of their feet (a style called "plantigrade"), not on their toes the way felines and canines do. They had small eyes and ears, a keen sense of smell, and barely a hint of a tail. They were the bears, eight of which survived to modern times: the sloth bear, sun bear, spectacled bear, giant panda, Asian black bear, North American black bear, polar bear, and the grizzly or brown bear.

The brown bear, the most aggressive and adaptable of the clan, spread throughout Europe and Asia and even into northern Africa. Tundra, plains, mountains, semi-desert—it didn't make much difference. The brown bear went where it wanted and did what it willed. Then, about 50,000 years ago, the brown bear colonized North America by strolling some 55 miles (88.5 km) across the Bering Land Bridge—the strip of dry terrain that once connected Asia and Alaska, providing a travel corridor for all manner of migrating wildlife. From Alaska, the bruin worked its way south and east until it occupied most of the western half of the continent.

Much confusion has swirled around the naming of the great brown bear. For starters, naturalists and biologists often become either "lumpers" or "splitters." Lumpers focus on similarities among animals and tend to come up with fewer classifications. Splitters look for differences and are more likely to separate wild creatures

Explorers like Lewis and Clark and many early North American settlers considered grizzlies a threat to their safety and livestock. (Photo © Gary Schultz)

Brown bears the world over are all members of the same species, Ursus arctos. *(Photo © Gary Schultz)*

into many groups. In addition, it used to be that just about anyone with a field journal and a little training in Latin could come up with a new moniker for an animal based on where it was sighted, what it was eating, or, seemingly, which way the wind was blowing. At one time, various folks had designated nearly 100 different North American brown bear species, each with its own scientific name, as well as descriptive common names—the Black Hills grizzly, Arizona grizzly, high-brow grizzly, industrious grizzly, strange grizzly, big-toothed grizzly, and on and on.

The nomenclature has since settled down considerably. Current thinking holds that all brown bears in the world are of the same species, *Ursus arctos*. In Latin, *Ursus* (the genus) means "bear," and *arctos* (the species) suggests a northern domicile. So, the entire cadre of big northerly bruins—be they in Canada, Scandinavia, Russia, or the United States—are *Ursus arctos*.

There are several subspecies of brown bears in Eurasia, but in North America scientists make only one additional distinction, dividing the clan into the subspecies *Ursus arctos horribilis* (originally named for the fear they struck in people) and *Ursus arctos middendorffi* (named for a Russian zoologist). The *middendorffi* bears live on a handful of islands off the southwestern coast of Alaska and are commonly called Kodiak brown bears, after the name of the largest of the islands. Kodiaks typically are bigger than other brown bears. The *horribilis* bears constitute the rest of the family. They are commonly known as grizzlies.

Kodiaks are the largest members of the brown bear clan. Some males weigh in excess of 1,300 pounds (590 kg). (Photo © W. Perry Conway)

Incidentally, the name "grizzly"—which has no scientific standing—is somewhat fuzzy in origin. It may be the Anglicization of the Old French word *grisel*, which meant gray or grayish (referring to the bear's often silver-tipped hair). Or maybe it is a form of the English "grisly," a comment on the bear's ability to rip bodies apart. Regardless of the origins of the name, "grizzly" is restricted to North America. Elsewhere in the world, the *Ursus arctos* are usually referred to simply as "brown bears."

These adaptive animals once thrived from the forests of southern Europe to the plains of central Asia to the near-desert of the Middle East to spruce-and-fir Siberian Taiga. In North America, grizzlies historically roamed

Grizzlies had already lived in North America for millennia when the first humans arrived about 11,000 years ago. (Photo © Duane Sept)

from Mexico to the Arctic Ocean and from the Pacific Ocean across the Great Plains, as far east as Iowa. They were most numerous in what is now Alaska and Canada, but in the contiguous states, 20 states west of the Mississippi River had grizzlies, possibly as many as 100,000 of them—10,000 in California alone. Why grizzlies did not inhabit the eastern half of the continent remains something of a mystery, as they had no enemies to speak of

and food was plentiful there. Some biologists and historians speculate that the big bears were in the process of colonizing points eastward when they ran into the buzz saw of westward-advancing European settlement.

Europeans did not make the North American grizzly's acquaintance until just a few centuries ago. No one knows for sure which conquistador first encountered the grizzly. It was likely either Álvar Núñez Cabeza de Vaca, who explored what is today Texas and northern Mexico between 1527 and 1536, or Francisco Vásquez de Coronado, who passed through much of the American Southwest and southern Midwest between 1540 and 1542.

The grizzly's name refers, in part, to its sometimes grayish color. One of its other nicknames is "silvertip." (Photo © Steven Nourse)

Neither adventurer wrote of a large and fearsome bear, but grizzlies were plentiful and probably hard to miss. A century later, French explorers and missionaries ran into grizzlies in present-day Manitoba, and in the 1690s, a Hudson's Bay Company employee in Saskatchewan, Henry Kelsey, probably became the first English-speaking person to lay eyes on griz and the first Caucasian to record the killing of a North American grizzly bear. However, it would be another century before Meriwether Lewis and William Clark, in their exploration of the American West in the early 1800s, called serious attention to the bear and collected specimens for scientific study.

The journals of Lewis and Clark abound with thrilling tales of grizzly encounters, narrow escapes, and—often—dead bears. One of the most interesting adventures unfolded near the present-day location of Great Falls, Montana. Lewis, exploring on his own ahead of the main party, shot a bison. Intent on watching the animal fall, he neglected to reload his muzzleloader or to notice the grizzly that had approached to within 20 steps of him. With no time now for loading, Lewis retreated toward the nearest tree, which stood 300 yards (275 m) distant. The enraged bear charged, forcing the explorer to switch to Plan B, which in this case meant jumping into the Missouri River. If the bear had to attack while swimming, Lewis reasoned, he (Lewis) might have some chance of surviving. Lewis splashed waist deep into the water, then turned to fight off the grizzly with his spontoon, a short, shafted pikelike weapon and a rather meager defense for such circumstances. The grizzly reached the water's edge, then—to Lewis's considerable relief and bewilderment—wheeled around and raced off.

This bear was more fortunate than many encountered by Lewis and Clark; their party killed 43 grizzlies during the expedition's three-year trek across the West. Despite the carnage, Lewis's documentation of the big bear's appearance, behavior, and range constituted the first scientific data on the grizzly. This information led naturalist George Ord in 1815 to christen the animal *Ursus horribilis*, which was later modified to *Ursus arctos horribilis*.

As the inevitable stream of pioneers flowed westward, the grizzly's fortunes began to fade. Unlike Native Americans, this new biped possessed the necessary weapons—primarily the repeating rifle—to dominate the previously indomitable grizzly. Ranchers feared for their sheep and cattle, farmers for their barnyard creatures, and parents for their children—and for themselves. In their estimation, the grizzly served no useful purpose while presenting considerable danger, an opinion that spelled the bruin's death sentence. So, with traps, guns, and poisons, the settlers set about to rid the land of this menace. To them, it made no difference whatsoever that most grizzlies lived quiet lives away from people and domestic animals.

To be sure, some grizzlies did on occasion kill livestock and even people. A few learned to wreak considerable havoc, and several regions had their own "rogue" or "renegade" bear that, according to local legend, delighted in waging a guerrilla war on people and their property. One Colorado bruin, dubbed Old Mose, supposedly killed 800 head of livestock, dozens of other domestic animals, and at least five men. But this bear also was accused of ravaging the countryside for 35 years, which would have made him a rather geriatric grizzly, so it is unlikely all of the crimes attributed to the bear were actually committed by Old Mose. Another stock-killing grizzly, known as Old Ephraim, became quite a celebrity and today lies buried beneath its own tombstone in the Utah mountains. In many western locales, the name "Old Ephraim" eventually became synonymous with "grizzly."

Pitted against a vastly superior enemy, the great bears retreated from wherever humans chose to settle. Initially, the bears disappeared from the prairies, foothills, and river bottoms of the West, but survived in good numbers in rugged wilderness areas. Then, like lights blinking off one by one, grizzlies began to vanish from even the remote lands of most states. Texas lost its last grizzly around 1890, California in 1922, Oregon in 1931, Arizona

Grizzlies once roamed across much of western North America. Today, they are abundant only in Alaska and Canada. (Photo © Alissa Crandall)

in 1935, and on and on.

Today, grizzlies in the Lower 48 occupy only about 2 percent of their original domain, and even that has been chopped by humans into unconnected islands of habitat. South of the Canadian border, only five isolated populations remain that together probably do not contain more than 1,000 of the big bears. (Grizzlies are difficult to census, so all population figures are estimates.) The five populations in the contiguous states are:

● Northern Continental Divide. About 9,600 square miles (25,000 sq. km) along the continent's backbone in northern Montana. This includes Glacier National Park and the Bob Marshall Wilderness. With between 400 and 600 grizzlies, this is by far the largest population.

● Yellowstone National Park. Two hundred or so grizzlies roam 9,500 square miles (24,700 sq. km) in the park and surrounding territory in Wyoming, Montana, and Idaho.

● Selkirk. About 1,000 square miles (2,600 sq. km) in rugged northern Idaho with perhaps 35 grizzlies. The population is named after the mountain range.

● Cabinet-Yaak. Named for a mountain range and a river in northwest Montana, this 2,600-square-mile (6,800-sq.-km) ecosystem has 15 to 20 grizzlies.

● North Cascades. A few grizzlies remain in this northwest Washington mountain range.

Grizzly status elsewhere on the continent is much better. Alaska is home to perhaps 40,000 (Kodiak brown bears and grizzlies combined), and Canada has another 25,000 or so grizzlies—primarily in British Columbia, Alberta, the Yukon, and the Northwest Territories.

Many Eurasian nations have at least a few bears left. Probably about a total of 100 browns survive in Spain, France, and Italy. Scandinavia has several hundred, Romania a few thousand, and the nations of the former Soviet Union several tens of thousands. Unknown numbers likely inhabit Turkey, Iraq, Afghanistan, China, North Korea, Japan, and other countries.

Ursus arctos, as a species, is not threatened with extinction, but its status has deteriorated immensely over the last century and a half, most acutely in the lower 48 states. Still, the grizzly remains a dominant feature of the natural landscape, as important a component of the wild world as it was eons ago when the first artists felt compelled to immortalize the great bears on cave walls.

In the lower 48 states, grizzlies exist in five separate populations that cumulatively probably do not contain more than 1,000 bears. (Photo © Alissa Crandall)

Making a Living

The grazing elk have let their guard down, and now the grizzly waits undetected in the timber just 80 yards (73 m) away. Suddenly, the bear bursts from its hiding place and charges like a locomotive onto the mountain meadow. Elk heads jerk upright, eyes wide with terror. Bodies wheel and hooves churn for purchase in the soft earth as the herd flees. But the grizzly has a running start and closes fast, watching for a cow elk crippled with age or a short-legged calf to fall behind, becoming separated from the herd. For 100 yards (90 m) or so, the grizzly maintains a deceivingly rapid stride and stays hot on the wapitis' heels, but no elk straggles, and soon the gap between predator and prey lengthens. Knowing it has lost this race, the grizzly slows to a walk. Soon, the giant paws, which a moment ago might have raked an elk to shreds, rip open an anthill, and the bear contents itself with lapping up insects.

A Native American aphorism says that when a leaf falls in the forest, the eagle sees it fall, the coyote hears it fall, and the grizzly smells it fall. That famous ursine nose is a good place to begin exploring just what makes a grizzly a grizzly. Above all else, this is an animal driven by the sense of smell. While people—and many other animals—use sight as the dominant sense in evaluating their environment, the grizzly uses its nose to know where to go, what to eat, whom to fight, and when to flee. Uncertain of what it is seeing or hearing, a grizzly may move downwind and confirm things with its nose. Often, a bear that encounters people—on a trail, for example—will rise on its hind legs. While this maneuver may also afford a better view, it likely is done primarily to enhance olfaction.

A ranger in Glacier National Park once encountered such a standing grizzly—at rather close range. Knowing the bear would likely head for the brush once it positively identified him as human, the ranger picked up a fist-sized rock, rubbed it in his armpit, and tossed it forward for the bruin to smell. Perhaps the man's adrenaline was flowing. Perhaps he was even closer to the bear than he thought. Whatever the reason, the rock did not roll to the bear's feet as intended, but rather thumped the animal solidly in the chest. "The loudest sound I ever heard," the ranger later called the thud. The grizzly, however, was not offended. It fell to all fours, sniffed the rock, and departed.

Some grizzlies become expert fishers. They do best when anadromous species, like salmon, migrate in large numbers. (Photo © D. R. Fernandez and M. L. Peck)

According to Andy Russell, famed Canadian adventurer and wilderness devotee, a grizzly's sense of smell is as big an improvement over a bloodhound's as the bloodhound's is over a human's. Reports suggest that grizzlies can follow the olfactory beacon emanating from a rotting elk carcass or a can of human garbage for up to 2 miles (3.2 km).

The grizzly's primary tool for gathering information is its nose. Rising on its hind legs may provide a better sniff. (Photo © Gary Schultz)

The bear's other senses are only so-so, however, at least in comparison with the extremely keen vision and hearing found in much of the rest of the wild world. Such things are tough to measure, but informed guesses say the bear's sight may approximate a human's, while its hearing is probably a bit better, including the ability to hear high-pitched sounds a person cannot detect.

Grizzlies range in color from black through a myriad shades of brown into reddish hues and even blond. Throw in the gray flecking that gives many of these bears that so-called grizzled look (and the nickname "silvertip"), and grizzly colors comprise a virtual rainbow. Black is uncommon, but it occurs often enough to keep people from jumping to the conclusion that the inky bruin eating their sandwiches is a relatively harmless black bear. (And, of course, black bears come in a variety of hues, too). Sibling cubs can vary widely in color—like the trio that was described as "one chocolate, one orange, and one lemon." Grizzly pelage is long and thick, with a softer, finer underfur. In the spring and early summer, grizzlies molt and often take on a somewhat ragged appearance.

Grizzly heft varies widely with gender, age, and food supply—ranging among adults from under 200 pounds (91 kg) for a female eking a living from inland alpine habitat, to more than 1,000 pounds (450 kg) for a male coastal grizzly or Kodiak brown bear fueled by lots of fish. A few of these Alaskan behemoths may even top 1,300 pounds (590 kg). But the average weight range is 400 to 800 pounds (180–360 kg) for adult grizzly males

The great bear's pelage ranges from black to blond. Grizzlies as dark as this one are actually rather rare. (Photo © Gary Schultz)

and considerably less for females. A big grizzly might stand 4 feet (1.2 m) tall at the shoulder and measure 8 feet (2.4 m) from nose to tail.

These bears are amazingly strong, capable of snapping off trees 6 inches (15 cm) in diameter and dislodging huge boulders from the ground. Grizzlies represent the epitome of muscled power, the culmination of nature's quest to create a supreme creature. Their jaws are particularly potent. One observer tells of listening from a distance as a grizzly family ate an elk, the bone-crunching sounds reminding him of a child eating hard candy. An oft-quoted maxim holds that a grizzly can kill a cow (or elk or caribou or other large ungulate) with a single blow from a front paw.

No, grizzlies can't walk on water, but on land they may hit 35 mph (56 kph). (Photo © David Welling)

In his book *In the Path of the Grizzly*, Alan Carey relates a couple prime examples of the great strength of the grizzly. Carey writes of a Glacier National Park naturalist who watched a grizzly and a wolverine feeding together on the carcass of a pack mule that had died in the backcountry. The odd couple got along well enough until the wolverine—one of the strongest creatures on earth relative to size—got a little too close. The grizzly glanced at the wolverine, then gave it a half-hearted backhand shot with its left forepaw. It was, by grizzly standards, not much of a blow, but the wolverine reeled backward, dead from a broken neck. And in Yellowstone National Park, a maintenance worker observed a grizzly attempting to pull an elk carcass (probably weighing at least 500 pounds/227 kg) up a riverbank. After the grizzly twice lost its grip and the elk slipped back into the water, the bear appeared to become agitated, got below the carcass, and with its front paws threw the elk over the 6-foot (1.8-m) bank onto level ground.

Grizzlies may appear slow and lumbering, but try racing one to the nearest tree, and you'll quickly come to a different conclusion. A grizzly can most likely outpace a racehorse over a short distance, which means humans stand no chance whatever of defeating griz in a foot race. (The standing joke among hikers in grizzly country is

It surprises many people to learn that most grizzlies, like this Canadian bruin, spend a lot of their time grazing on a variety of grasses, sedges, flowers, and other plants. (Photo © Duane Sept)

Grizzlies, like this bear in British Columbia's Khutzeymateen Valley, often follow streams in their perpetual search for food. (Photo © Adrian Dorst)

that you don't need to be faster than griz as long as you can outrun at least one of your colleagues.) Under the radar gun, a grizzly at full throttle would likely register 35 or so miles per hour (56 kph) over a short distance.

Although grizzlies clearly belong in the order Carnivora (carnivores or meat eaters), their predatory skills do not approach those of, say, wolves. It also surprises many people to learn that grizzlies are primarily vegetarians. It hardly fits the animal's fierce reputation, but the majority of grizzlies spend most of their time grazing. Consequently, grizzly teeth are less suited to ripping meat than are those of other large predators. A grizzly's 2-inch-long (5-cm-long) canines are indeed formidable, but its molars and premolars are designed more for grinding plants than slicing meat. In all, the grizzly has 42 pearly whites.

Long front claws make excellent digging tools. Subterranean delicacies include insects, ground squirrels, and marmots. (Photo © Tom Walker)

The big bear, however, got into vegetarianism too late (evolutionarily speaking) to develop the many-chambered stomach and attendant bacteria that make ruminants such efficient consumers of plants. While elk, deer, and other cud chewers can squeeze adequate sustenance from minimal amounts of the bleakest fare, grizzlies must eat large quantities of vegetation *and* consume the plant life at its seasonal nutritional peak.

This means, for example, concentrating on emerging lowland grasses and flowers in the spring, plants at higher elevations during the summer, and berries in the fall. Specific botanical menu items include dandelions, shooting stars, dog-tooth violets, clover, whitebark pine nuts, huckleberries, strawberries, buffalo berries, soapberries, salmonberries, mountain ash berries, raspberries, cow parsnip, pea vine, horsetails, and mountain sorrel. There are many others. Subterranean vegetative items include roots, bulbs, and tubers, and the great bear is not averse to digging in the ground for insects as well. One telltale sign of grizzly presence is a mountain meadow with dinner-plate-sized chunks of sod scattered about and rocks as big as beach balls rolled from their beds.

The overall grizzly diet is almost without end: fish, clams, carrion of all kinds, human garbage, tree cambium, honey, fruit, nuts, and virtually anything else animal or vegetable. "To [the grizzly] almost everything is food except granite," commented the American naturalist John Muir a century ago. Muir went on to say: "A sheep or a wounded deer or a pig he eats warm, about as quickly as a boy eats a buttered muffin; or should the meat be a month old, it is still welcomed with tremendous relish. After so gross a meal as this, perhaps the next will be strawberries and clover, or raspberries with mushrooms and nuts, or puckery acorns and chokecherries. And as if fearing that anything eatable in all his domain should escape being eaten, he breaks into cabins to look after sugar, dried apples, bacon, etc."

Although grizzlies rarely kill healthy ungulates, they often dine on large animals that have died from other causes, such as this moose. (Photo © Tom Walker)

When it comes to food, grizzlies have amazing memories, returning year after year like Capistrano's cliff swallows to previous feasting sites. Streams with migrating fish often become a regular stop on the grizzly dining tour. Perhaps the best-known ursine fishing hole is Alaska's McNeil River, where up to 60 grizzlies at a time annually assemble to harvest spawning salmon. Techniques vary. One griz may gracefully sweep fish from the water with a forepaw. Another might pin its quarry to the bottom. Another may prefer the jaw lunge, like a kid bobbing for apples. One very patient fishergriz even learned to pluck salmon from the air as they jumped over obstacles.

Another annual treat occurs high in Yellowstone's mountains each summer as millions of army cutworm moths emigrate from the Great Plains. When the insect horde hits the park high country, the bears have a gastronomic field day, slurping down the highly nutritional moths like winged dinner mints—perhaps 20,000 per bear per day. Containing 72 percent fat and 28 percent protein, the moths are an excellent dietetic choice, providing up to 90 percent of the summer's sustenance for some grizzlies.

As predators, grizzlies are most effective against burrowing animals such as ground squirrels and marmots. Powerful forelegs and strong claws make this bear one of the most capable diggers in nature, as many deceased rodents have discovered the hard way. A grizzly in hot pursuit of a ground squirrel can seem absolutely obsessed as it races from one burrow entrance to another, then digs furiously and sends football-sized rocks flying. More than one cub watching the action from the wrong position has been beaned with airborne tailings from mom's excavation. It often appears to the human eye that the bear must certainly burn more calories digging than it could possible acquire from its diminutive prey, but you have to assume the bear knows what it's doing. Or perhaps grizzlies engage in these furious hunts mostly for sport.

Bigger game is generally a tougher catch, as healthy hoofed creatures (elk, deer, caribou, moose, and the like) are normally able to escape most grizzly attacks. Although the bears do occasionally kill ungulates—usually the young, aged, or infirm—griz poses little threat to overall herd prosperity. Studies in Yellowstone—an area heavily populated with ungulates—suggest that each grizzly is likely to kill only one to six of these prey animals each year.

Much of the meat that finds its way into grizzly stomachs comes courtesy of winter kill, disease, wolf or cougar predation, or animals wounded by human hunters. Such carrion is an especially important part of the grizzly diet, particularly following the bears' emergence from their dens in spring. At any time of year, grizzlies value these fetid treasures highly, and anyone or anything coming between a griz and its store of rotting meat is likely in big trouble.

In the fall, berry bounty becomes extremely important, as the bear races to add the thick layer of fat that will nourish it through the winter. Art Pearson, a grizzly researcher in Canada's Yukon Territory, studied grizzly berry consumption. Knowing that soapberries, the primary species eaten by bears in the area, contain only one seed each, he counted seeds in typical bear scats (by any measure, a tough way to make a living), then multiplied by the probable number of daily defecations. Amazingly, he concluded that during peak season a grizzly might eat 200,000 soapberries in a day. Whatever the menu, an adult grizzly on a successful summer day may consume 30 pounds (13.6 kg) of food, and in the feeding frenzy prior to fall denning, that figure may triple.

Grizzlies are not particularly social animals. Females, of course, travel with their young, but the majority of others keep to themselves most of the time. Since these big bears are extremely powerful and not hesitant about attacking their own kind, they have evolved certain behaviors to help convey intentions and keep intraspecific bloodletting to a minimum. This body language is too complex to detail here, but it involves the position of the back, head, neck, mouth, and ears; bluff charges; walking posture; eye contact; and an assortment of sounds. After a few encounters, each member of the grizzly society knows pretty much where it ranks in relation to the others, and roaring battles are rare. Generally, an older male dominates, cubs reside at the bottom of the pecking order, and other bears are arranged in between. Females with cubs become more aggressive and tend to rise in relative rank.

The image of the loner grizzly has exceptions, however. A female with cubs can be amenable to having other such families around, creating the kind of situation that might be called friendship if they were humans. Also, when food is truly abundant—such as at Yellowstone National Park's erstwhile garbage dumps and during some fish migrations—grizzlies can be surprisingly tolerant of their kind. In these venues, the dominance hierarchy may determine who gets the choicest offal or the most productive fishing hole. When clashes do occur, bluff and bluster usually prevail over claws-on battle.

About the only other time unrelated bears tolerate one another is during the grizzly social event of the season—mating. In May or June, the reproductive urge overrides all others, and sexually mature adults seek each other out for a relatively brief amorous en-

Grizzlies generally are loners. Gatherings like this occur only where food is extremely abundant. Migrating fish are the attraction here. (Photo © Kennan Ward)

counter. The female emits estrus odors, and the grizzly Lothario follows its nose to the lady's side. For several days, a grizzly pair may travel together, the male repeatedly testing his partner's readiness to copulate. Biologists suspect that the male's presence is required to trigger ovulation.

Courtship includes plenty of rubbing, licking, and other physical contact, even if it is nothing more than lying side by side. Gender-specific behaviors include the male's stiff-legged, swaggering walk and low-slung head and the female's cowering submission. Copulation itself lasts from five minutes to an hour and may be repeated several times over a few days. Once estrus ends, the two bears resume their very separate lives. If pregnancy has not occurred, the female may enter a second estrus a week or so later.

Where several grizzlies are present—such as at concentrated feeding sites—both males and females will seek multiple mates. Ever-possessive males in such situations often face the doubly strenuous task of mating with

Top: Fights between grizzlies may occur when females protect their young, males covet the same mate, or food ownership is in question. (Photo © Kennan Ward)
Bottom: Mating season is about the only time unrelated grizzlies actively seek each other out. (Photo © Tom Walker)

Female grizzlies are protective, nurturing mothers that allow cubs frequent access to their highly nutritional milk. (Photo © Kennan Ward)

as many females as possible while attempting to prevent their concubines from being equally promiscuous. Occasionally, competitions among males may turn violent—and even deadly. An autopsy of the loser of one such battle revealed 89 puncture wounds, a 2-inch (5-cm) hole in the chest, broken ribs, a broken shoulder, dislocated neck, broken nose bridge, and crushed skull.

Compared to many other mammals, grizzly reproduction is torturously slow. A female is often four or five years old (possibly even eight or nine) when she mates for the first time, and thereafter will likely produce only two or three cubs every three to four years. (Cubs can remain with their mother for two years or more, effectively taking her out of mating circulation.) Statistically, half her offspring will be males, most of which are unnecessary for the perpetuation of the population, because one male can impregnate several females. And some of the six or so female cubs she produces during her lifetime will not live long enough to breed. Ergo, it is not unusual for a female grizzly to raise to adulthood only one or two female offspring over her entire 15- to 20-year life span.

Consequently, grizzly cubs are valuable commodities, and mothers defend their offspring with singular ferocity. Female grizzlies with cubs are, perhaps, the most fearsome animals on earth, and even adult males—themselves no slouches when it comes to combative vigor—often defer to an enraged mother grizzly. Motherly protection notwithstanding, adult males kill some cubs (possibly to bring their mother into estrus sooner), and accidents, disease, poaching, and malnutrition claim others. Up to one third of all cubs perish before reaching the age of two.

Mother grizzlies take parenting seriously, fiercely protecting their offspring one moment, cuffing them in discipline the next, and frolicking with them the next. Cubs nurse four or five times each day for several minutes to supplement the solid food they begin eating early in life. Many cubs continue to nurse into their second summer, and a few even do so until they are two and a half years old and nearly as big as their mother. Grizzly milk is exceptionally rich, with a fat content of about 30 percent, compared to 3 percent for cow's milk.

By its first autumn, a cub (born in midwinter) may weigh 60 to 100 pounds (27–45 kg). For the most part, young grizzlies are as they have been portrayed in countless television programs—playful, roly-poly, irresistibly appealing to humans, and incessantly curious. They will learn a lot about grizzlyhood from their mother, but the urge to investigate every log, rock, mound, and bush appears innate and universal.

Cubs typically remain with their mother until they are in their second or sometimes even third summer. This means, of course, that they den together once or even twice. Often, the family breakup occurs when the

female enters estrus again and males start coming around. In a scene that tugs at human heartstrings, the female often gruffly drives off her cubs, which naturally are reluctant to leave their gravy-train mother-defender behind. Emancipation is one of the most perilous times for a young grizzly, suddenly devoid of its mother's protection, without a home range of its own, and not yet fully educated about life's perils. Newly emancipated sibling cubs may travel together for a time (and even den together for one winter), but eventually they will split up, as each pursues its own life as an adult grizzly bear.

Historically, grizzlies had few life-threatening enemies outside of their own kind and Native Americans, who probably did not kill many of the big bears. Perhaps wolves and cougars occasionally took a grizzly cub from an inattentive mother, and a bison or bull elk battling for its life might rarely land a lucky horn or antler and kill a bear, but most grizzlies probably died nonviolent deaths. Common causes of mortality included old age, malnutrition, or inadequate fat reserves during hibernation. That pattern changed dramatically, however, with the arrival of European immigrants and their weapons.

Although blatant bear slaughter ended long ago, most grizzly deaths today are still tied to human presence. Bears that attack people—or even threaten unprovoked attacks—may pay with their lives. Poachers and grizzly haters illegally kill bears, and authorities are sometimes forced to eliminate a grizzly that repeatedly bothers livestock or hangs around dwellings. Other mortality borders on the bizarre. Just outside Glacier National Park's southern boundary, Burlington Northern trains seem to have a habit of derailing and spilling considerable quantities of grain. Grizzlies come to dine on this windfall, and since 1987 at least nine of them have been hit by trains and killed (sometimes because the fermented grain made them tipsy).

In the Northern Continental Divide and Yellowstone populations combined, 34 grizzlies were known to have perished in 1995. Thirteen died due to management actions (usually removing problem bears), seven were killed illegally, three were shot by people acting in self-defense, two were hit by trains, three were electrocuted, and only three died of natural causes (plus three for which cause of death could not be determined).

But just as humans are responsible for most grizzly deaths, so do we hold the key to the great bear's future. If people permit, the grizzly may indeed continue to make a living the only way it knows how—by pulling down an occasional elk, digging furiously in the earth, and eating everything but granite.

The strong bond between a female and her offspring may extend into the cubs' third year. The eventual family breakup usually occurs when the female enters estrus and becomes more interested in mating than mothering. (Photo © Henry H. Holdsworth)

The Big Sleep

The icy blasts penetrate even the thick coat of grizzled hair, and snow borne on the shotgun wind stings the great bear's face. The grizzly's chest heaves with labored breath as it struggles uphill through the deepening snow. Overhead, the sky crouches low, gray, and heavy. The bear knows the time has come. Finally it arrives at a huge fir tree. A few swipes from giant paws sweep away the snow to reveal an opening beneath the tree. The grizzly turns and looks once more down the valley, but there is no other animal within sight. The bruin drops to its belly, wriggles through the seemingly too small entrance, and in a moment disappears into the womb of the earth.

Quite literally, a grizzly may sleep half its life away. Somehow, the hibernation that appears appropriate for small, subterranean creatures like prairie dogs and ground squirrels seems oddly out of place for the grizzly. But each autumn the great bear obeys instincts honed over countless generations and seeks out a den for the winter. What follows is one of nature's miracles.

Bears developed hibernation as a way to circumvent winter food shortages and prevent starvation. Ineffective as a predator and with a digestive system ill-equipped for wringing sustenance from poor-quality vegetation, the grizzly simply opted to survive winter by not eating at all.

The hibernation process begins with the ripening of berries in late summer, as well as an abundance of certain other foods. The grizzly's normally robust appetite kicks into overdrive, and the bear may feed almost around the clock in an attempt to sate the insatiable. In just a few weeks, an adult grizzly may put on 100 pounds (45 kg), mostly in the form of a fat layer up to 10 inches (25 cm) thick. It is this surplus that will fuel the ursine engine through the long months of winter.

When food supplies start to wane, each grizzly (or grizzly family, in the case of a female with cubs) searches for an appropriate den. Hollow trees and natural caves occasionally become dens, but most grizzlies prefer to excavate their own. Normally, they dig their dens on fairly steep hillsides (25 degrees to as steep as 60 degrees) and in places that receive abundant snowfall. Good snow cover is important because it plugs the den entrance and keeps cold drafts out, and bears seem instinctively to know where the deep snow will accumulate. The

Grizzlies may encounter snow in the spring and fall, but they spend most of the cold season snuggled away in a den. (Photo © Kennan Ward)

elevation and compass orientation of grizzly dens vary among different bear populations but remain rather consistent within a given group. For example, Yellowstone's grizzlies typically den at elevations between 7,800 and 9,200 feet (2,375–4,175 m) on forested, north-facing slopes.

The base of a large tree is a favorite denning spot, probably because the tree's roots help stabilize the soil and prevent the den roof from collapsing. Far from elaborate, a typical den consists of a small opening, a short passageway (generally 1 to 5 feet/.45–1.5 m), and a sleeping chamber not much larger than the bear itself. Often, the chamber lies a little higher than the tunnel, most likely to prevent water from collecting where the bear sleeps. Typically, the bear drags branches and grass into the den to create a bed filled with small air pockets, which serve to insulate the sleeper from the ground. Although bears use some dens a second time, most grizzlies excavate anew each year. In October or November, the grizzly takes that last look around and wriggles into its berth.

Scientists don't yet fully understand what triggers the autumn feeding frenzy, den digging, and eventual hibernation. Declining photoperiod (the number of daylight hours) almost certainly plays a part. Cooler fall temperatures may as well. Also, certain evidence suggests that the arrival of autumn's first big snow is the signal that sends bears into their dens, suggesting that the bruins somehow know the drifts will hide their tracks and cover the tunnel entrance. Another possible trigger is the declining food supply typical of late autumn. Bears that experience no seasonal deterioration of their provender (such as those in zoos) often do not hibernate. And new evidence from Glacier National Park suggests that some grizzlies may interrupt—or even forego—hibernation when wolves and cougars kill enough winter prey to satisfy an ursine appetite. (A grizzly usually can appropriate a kill over the objections of the original owner or owners, even a wolf pack.) Most grizzlies, however, pass the winter in slumber.

Inside the den, bear biology and chemistry change dramatically, creating a kind of metabolic magic. A normal summer heart rate while sleeping of 40 or 50 beats per minute drops to 8 or 10. Oxygen consumption declines by 50 percent. Body temperature, however, falls only slightly, from a normal 100 degrees Fahrenheit (38°C) to perhaps 90 degrees (32°C). Incredibly, the hibernating grizzly will go several months without eating, drinking, urinating, or defecating. However, since the bear's body temperature remains near normal, the grizzly continues to burn plenty of fatty fuel—4,000 to 8,000 calories per day for a large bear.

The hibernation process begins with the ripening of berries. For weeks, the bears feed almost continuously to accumulate fat, the fuel that will sustain them through the winter. (Photo © Robert E. Barber)

In other hibernators, such as ground squirrels, body temperature descends nearly to the ambient level, the heart all but stops beating, and the animals become stonelike and virtually impossible to arouse. Because bears maintain a relatively high body temperature and are easily awakened, they were long considered not to be true hibernators. Scientists have reevaluated this matter, however, and now regard grizzlies and their kin as hibernatory.

Some scientists think the season's first major snowfall may be the trigger that finally sends grizzlies into their dens for the winter. (Photo © Gary Schultz)

Interestingly, the rodent hibernators regularly wake up to eat stored food, urinate, and defecate, activities that are not a part of ursine hibernation. During these arousals, their temperature and heartbeat rise to normal levels.

Although the hibernating grizzly consumes no fluids for months and actually loses considerable water in exhaled breath, it does not become dehydrated, and its volume of blood (and other fluids) does not decrease. For weeks on end, this huge animal gets all the moisture it needs from the metabolization of fat. Each fat cell converted to energy produces a little water as a byproduct, moisture the bear reuses.

The treatment of wastes is even more remarkable. Since the bear consumes no food, there are no solids to eliminate, but the bear's kidneys do not go on vacation. In fact, they continue removing a nitrogenous compound called *urea* from the blood. Urea is a byproduct of normal protein metabolism, a process required to maintain blood glucose at adequate levels (metabolism solely of fat does not create enough glucose). Most mammals, including humans and bears (when not in hibernation), could survive only a few days without removing the poisonous urea from the blood and excreting it in urine. But a hibernating grizzly does not urinate—for months. So how does it prevent uremic poisoning and death? Somehow—the exact mechanism is still a mystery—the grizzly breaks down the toxic urea and turns the resulting nitrogen back into new protein, literally reversing the starvation process. Bears are the only animals capable of performing this ultimate feat of recycling, a trick doctors would love to duplicate in people with kidney failure. The bears, however, are keeping the secret to themselves.

For weeks at a time, the hibernating grizzly may not even roll over, although its sleep is light, and it remains capable of quick arousal and vigorous defense against any creature so unwise as to enter the den. Occasionally, the grizzly awakens, rearranges its bedding, grooms, then dozes off again. Infrequently, a winter warm spell may inspire a hibernating grizzly to leave the den and wander about for a while, but invariably the den looks better than the largely foodless winter world, and the bruin returns. Depending on the circumstances—mostly meteorological—grizzly hibernation may be as short as ten weeks or as long as seven months.

But there is yet another marvel of nature taking place in some bear dens. Grizzlies mate in late spring, and one to three of the female's eggs are fertilized at that time. The embryos grow for a brief period, then enter a state of suspended animation. For nearly half a year, they float freely in the female's uterus, their fate uncertain. If autumn food is scarce, nature may call off reproduction for the year, and the female's body will absorb the microscopic embryos. This frees the female from the rigors of motherhood, perhaps ensuring her survival to breed again in better times. Some biologists even speculate that this reproductive *decision* is not an all-or-nothing proposition, that the number of cubs produced (as opposed to the simpler question of whether there will be cubs at all) is tied to the female's nutritional health. A food-filled fall might mean three embryos will make it; a mediocre or average autumn might result in only one or two surviving.

About the time the female reaches her maximum autumn weight, the embryos end their dormancy, attach to the uterine wall, and begin growing again. Called delayed implantation, this process is also practiced by several other mammalian species, including mink, bats, and kangaroos. Scientists think it may have evolved in bears as a way to keep the rigorous and sometimes violent mating season far removed from the crucial autumn feeding period. Also, if the embryos were to grow steadily from the moment of conception, the cubs would likely be too large at birth for the female to nurse successfully during the foodless months inside the den.

While the female sleeps, the embryos mature, and in midwinter, as blizzards rage above ground, she awakens long enough to give birth—often to twins, but singles and triplets are not uncommon. With a real gestation of just six or eight weeks, the rat-sized newborn cubs weigh only about a pound (.45 kg) apiece and measure barely a foot (30 cm) from nose to tail. Compared to the size of the mother, grizzly newborns are among the smallest in all of mammaldom. They also are toothless, covered with almost invisibly fine hair, and have eyes that will remain closed a month or more. For several additional weeks, the grizzly family snoozes, the cubs growing rapidly on the fat-rich formula available at their mother's teats. Incredibly, the female grizzly meets the considerable demands of pregnancy and nursing without consuming a morsel of food or sip of drink.

In the spring (between March and June, depending on location and weather), something tells the grizzly to leave the den. Perhaps it is the increasing amount of sunlight creeping into the chamber, but more likely some sort of biological alarm clock goes off. Usually, males are the first to emerge, followed in order by cubless females, females with yearling cubs, and females with newborns. (Autumn entrance into dens often is the reverse of this sequence, with pregnant females denning first.) Normally, the adult grizzly that steps from its den into the spring sunshine has lost from 15 to 40 percent of its autumn weight, but is otherwise in remarkably good shape. Its muscles have not atrophied from disuse. Its bones have not lost vital calcium. Its lean tissue has not diminished. And at least one part of the grizzly anatomy has improved measurably during hibernation; front claws worn down during the previous summer's digging are now renewed and ready for action.

This female and her nearly grown cub will probably den on one of the distant slopes. (Photo © Henry H. Holdsworth)

You would think a bear that had fasted for months would devour anything that looked like food, but this often is not the case. Many grizzlies exit the den with some fat remaining and only an average appetite. Also, it may take time for the considerable metabolic changes of hibernation to reverse themselves and allow griz to experience real hunger again. As for the newborns, they are furry toddlers weighing 5 or 6 pounds (2.3–2.7 kg) at emergence from the den, still less than most human infants weigh at birth. By midsummer, however, a cub may hit 50 pounds (23 kg), en route to the even greater autumn heft that will allow it to slumber away the following winter at its mother's side.

Top: Occasionally, a grizzly will leave its den long before spring. Finding the world cold and bereft of food, these early emergers usually resume hibernation after a brief taste of winter. (Photo © Gary Schultz)
Bottom: These cubs were born in midwinter while their mother hibernated. The family of three will den together when winter returns. (Photo © Alissa Crandall)

Close Encounters of the Ursine Kind

The blond grizzly ambles down the hillside, here and there digging up a wildflower snack or rolling a log over and lapping up the insects beneath. At the worn hiking trail, the bear pauses, perhaps to read the olfactory messages left by previous passers-by. By coincidence, two hikers, a man and a woman in their twenties, round a bend 80 yards (73 m) away, see the grizzly, and freeze. At a brisk pace, the grizzly approaches the terrified couple, who—whether out of paralyzing fear or good sense—stand their ground. The bear's ears are up and alert, not laid back in attack posture; it is walking, not running; its head rides high—all signs that the grizzly might be simply curious, not aggressive. The bear approaches to within 20 feet (6 m), stops, and turns sideways on the trail. For a fleeting moment, the grizzly looks at the petrified humans, then—apparently assured they constitute no threat, or perhaps concluding they aren't worth the trouble— steps downslope off the trail and disappears into the forest. The only sound louder than the bear's brushy exit is the twin pounding of human hearts.

Once you see a grizzly up close, you don't soon forget it. The image becomes etched in your memory, the way you remember what you were doing when you learned World War II had ended, John Kennedy had been shot, or the space shuttle *Challenger* had exploded. For years after you encounter a grizzly, you parade that memory anew before acquaintances whenever the subject of bears arises. And because of the aura surrounding the grizzly, the account likely needs no embellishment. Grizzlies are that awesome.

They're also potentially dangerous to people, which adds an entirely new perspective to the bear-human relationship and a voluminous library to the grizzly chronicle. Tales of grizzly encounters have been around for centuries, and just about everyone who lives or vacations in grizzly country has heard any number of mauling accounts. Like that of Sarah Muller, who went hiking one July in the Slough Creek area of Yellowstone National Park. When she came upon a mother grizzly with cubs, the female attacked, furiously biting and clawing the woman. Thirty interminable minutes later, friends on horseback found the 34-year-old Muller—one lung punctured and collapsed, seven ribs fractured, a broken arm, multiple punctures and cuts all over her body, and bleeding profusely. It took physicians 12 hours to treat her wounds. To her considerable credit, Muller pleaded with park authorities—successfully—to spare the bear's life.

One rule for hikers in bear country: Never share a swimming hole with a grizzly. (Photo © Kennan Ward)

Occasionally, individual grizzlies develop considerable reputations. History is full of such accounts, although many of these tales may have been exaggerated over time. Better documented is the more recent saga of the Giefer Grizzly. In 1975, Montana authorities captured and relocated a troublesome bear from the Giefer Creek area just south of Glacier National Park to the northwest part of the state. Perhaps dissatisfied with its new digs,

Hiking trails are the site of many grizzly-human encounters. Smart hikers make plenty of noise, watch for signs of bruin presence, and refrain from traveling alone. (Photo © Michael H. Francis)

the Giefer Grizzly, as the animal came to be called in the newspapers, went on a spree of breaking and entering that would have done any burglar proud. Nearly every week during the summer of 1976, a new report surfaced of the grizzly invading some cabin in this remote part of Montana. During one break-in, the bruin somehow removed its electronic radio-tracking collar, leaving the transmitter—perhaps for spite—on the cabin floor. In another case, the homeowner surmised that the bear had taken a nap in his bed. The bruin foiled numerous attempts at capture, and before taking a hiatus for denning that fall, amassed a rap sheet listing 19 forcible entries. Some folks, admiring any animal that could outwit legions of wardens and biologists, took to rooting for the Giefer Griz and even held a wake that fall when unfounded rumors of the grizzly's death were making the rounds. But the bear survived, and the following spring, property owners braced for a renewal of hostilities, but in April a hunter in Canada killed a bear whose ear tags positively identified it as the infamous Giefer Grizzly.

What is likely the most dramatic episode in modern ursine history occurred in Glacier National Park on an August night in 1967, when two grizzlies, in separate incidents 30 trail miles (48 km) apart, killed two young women camping in the backcountry. This incredible coincidence sparked banner headlines across the country, spawned a book (*Night of the Grizzlies* by Jack Olsen), and sent park authorities into a frenzy of self-examination. Since the park's inception in 1910, its hundreds of grizzlies had lived more or less in peace with the 16 million people that had visited the park over the years; then in one night two people died! What was going on there?

The upshot of all the post-incident scrutiny seemed to be a realization that grizzlies can indeed be dangerous, and people should do whatever they can to minimize the chances of an attack when in grizzly country. Since the 1967 tragedy, government officials at Glacier, Yellowstone, and Denali National Parks in the U.S., and Banff, Jasper, and Waterton Lakes National Parks in Canada, as well as other lands that are home to grizzlies, have emphasized educating hikers, campers, and other people venturing into grizzly habitat about the potential dangers from bears. Authorities have taken other measures, too, to reduce the likelihood of conflicts—such as closing garbage dumps in parks and enforcing clean-camp rules.

Still, a grizzly will, from time to time, maul or even kill a human. Since the start of record-keeping in 1906, grizzlies have taken about 50 lives in all of North America. The number of maulings, treeings, and other encounters is, of course, much higher. Generally, authorities will spare the offending animal's life if the incident resulted from a human mistake or was a normal bear reaction to circumstances it perceived as threatening. That is, a bear that has attacked a human likely will not be killed if the assault occurred because the person got too close, came between a female and her cubs, approached some juicy carrion, or surprised the grizzly on a trail. But a grizzly that drags a camper from a tent—provided the camper has taken appropriate precautions with food—may well be tracked down and killed.

Though rare, unprovoked attacks do occur. In the pre-dawn dark of September 25, 1995, a female grizzly and her cub accomplice thoroughly terrorized campers near Lake Louise in Canada's Banff National Park. At three different campsites, the bears ripped open tents and pulled sleeping tourists into the night. "It [the bear] grabbed my sleeping bag and ripped it straight off my body," said one victim. Six people—two each from Montana, Australia, and Germany—suffered injuries (none serious), and many other terrified campers, alerted by the victims' screams, fled to the safety of cars and buildings. Authorities could find no reason for the attacks, as all the victims had properly locked their food in special storage bins designed to prevent bear intrusions. The next evening, when two bears fitting the attackers' descriptions returned to the campground, officials captured and killed them.

What often gets lost in all the bear-attack headlines, however, is perspective. Surely, being mauled to death by a grizzly bear is a gruesome way to die. But does that danger merit more worry than other perils? Statistically, a person is more likely to perish—even in grizzly habitat—from a bee sting, a falling tree, lightning, drowning, hypothermia, or any number of other threats than from a bear attack. Anyone who parks at a trailhead in Glacier,

Female grizzlies with cubs can be the most dangerous animals on earth. (Photo © Gary Schultz)

Yellowstone, or Canada's Jasper National Park and hikes off into grizzlyland has already survived the most dangerous part of the trip—the car ride.

Most grizzlies have an innate wariness of humans. When people are nearby, bears invariably prefer to be elsewhere, and given a choice, they will usually go there. Every summer, many confrontations are avoided—unbeknownst to the humans—because the bears saw, heard, or smelled people coming and quietly slipped away. When tragic encounters do occur, it's usually because the person or people stumbled accidentally into a dangerous situation or failed to heed one or more of the canons of grizzly avoidance. Anyone who ventures on foot into grizzly habitat—and this certainly includes all hikers in Glacier, Yellowstone, Denali, and several Canadian national parks—should know the commandments for safety and survival in grizzly country:

Thou shalt not go quietly. Let griz know you're coming. Make noise. Talk loudly. Sing. Wear bear bells. Rattle a stone in a pop can.

Thou shalt avoid places of likely encounter. Stay out of thick brush, especially along streams. Avoid trails that provide a poor view of surrounding terrain. Keep away from carrion. Let the bears have the autumn berry patches.

Thou shalt not come betwixt a mother grizzly and her cubs. Female grizzlies are fierce defenders of their young.

When humans and grizzlies use the same areas, the potential for trouble always exists. (Photo © Alissa Crandall)

Thou shalt observe the signs of grizzly presence. Such as scat that approaches 2 inches (5 cm) in diameter, large rocks recently overturned, rotted wood torn apart, evidence of digging in meadows and other open places, and large paw prints with prominent claw marks. If you encounter any of these grizzly indicators, leave the area.

Thou shalt know basic grizzly body language. When you've encountered a bruin, direct eye contact and shouting are confrontational. When a grizzly turns its head sideways, it is a sign of submission and appeasement. Laying its ears back may mean an attack is imminent. A grizzly that rises on its hind legs is probably seeking better information, not getting ready to charge.

A grizzly standing on its hind legs is probably gathering information (via its eyes or nose), not getting ready to charge. (Photo © Alan and Sandy Carey)

Thou shalt not run. Like other predators, grizzlies tend to chase whatever flees. Stand your ground. Hit the ground, if necessary. Say some prayers. Wave your arms. Talk quietly to the bear. But do not run—unless you are absolutely *certain* you can beat the bear to a tall tree. If retreat is possible, do so slowly without turning your back to the bear.

One final word about grizzly safety. Researchers at the University of Montana tested a number of deterrents on grizzlies—everything from rock music to fireworks to a suddenly opened umbrella—invariably with poor results. In general, it is not easy to make a grizzly retreat. However, the big bear has been sent packing fairly reliably by a spray containing the stinging, burning essence of cayenne pepper. Many park rangers, hikers, bowhunters, and others now carry a can of such a spray on their belts. The product receiving the best reviews is called Counter Assault. It is nontoxic and does not cause any permanent harm to the sprayee.

Not long ago, Counter Assault likely saved the life of Montana bowhunter Bayne French. One autumn morning, French, 22, was hunting elk in the mountains when he came to a large thicket of alder, and rather than take the time to go around, he started into the copse. Almost immediately, he heard grunting and the sounds of something crashing through the brush on the slope above him, and French initially believed he had stumbled upon a bull elk. However, as the thrashing came closer and lost its elklike quality, French got nervous and

Grizzly cubs, like this Montana youngster, climb rather well. Adults, however, remain mostly on the ground. (Photo © Michael H. Francis)

readied his can of spray. Suddenly, the grizzly appeared, ripping large alders out by the roots as it approached. When the charging bear closed to within a dozen feet (3.7 m) or so, French fired a one-second burst of Counter Assault directly into the animal's face. Immediately, the bear slammed on the brakes, showering the hunter's legs and feet with dirt and forest duff. Then the bruin swapped ends and raced off.

Remember, though, that the spray is a last-ditch, after-the-prayers-are-said, when-all-else-fails weapon. To use it, you must have the courage to stand your ground and spray an irritant directly into the eyes and nose of an aggressive grizzly. Not everyone can do that. Ergo, if at all possible, it is much better to avoid getting that close to a grizzly in the first place.

For many people who find themselves in the presence of grizzlies, sanctuary may be as close as the nearest climbable tree. Although grizzly cubs occasionally go arboreal, adults generally cannot climb. They have the required strength, of course, but lack the curved claws necessary for purchase on a tree trunk. Black bears, having more curved claws, climb well at all ages. This raises the issue of species identification. The two bruins often occupy the same habitat, and any person making the sudden acquaintance of a bear would do well to know whether the creature is a grizzly or a black. One adage suggests that the best way to do this is to climb a tree. If the bruin comes up the tree after you, it's a black bear. If it rips the tree out of the ground, it's a grizzly.

This British Columbia bruin displays the front shoulder hump characteristic of grizzlies. Absence of such a hump likely means the animal is a black bear. (Photo © Duane Sept)

In reality, there are better routes to *Ursus* identification. First, forget color. Both species range all over the black-brown-tan map. Size can be definitive toward the extremes of the weight range; virtually all 700-pounders (318-kg) will be grizzlies and all adult 150-pounders (68-kg) will be black bears. But plenty of overlap exists in the middle, where a big black may outweigh a small grizzly. Few people know how to get a bear to stand on a scale, anyway.

Perhaps the best diagnostic feature is the large hump between the grizzly's front shoulders, which is absent for the most part in black bears. The hump, called the roach, is the musculature that drives the incredibly powerful grizzly front end, and the roach is usually visible at considerable distance. Another distinctive grizzly attribute is the dish-shaped contour of its face. In profile, the black bear's snout runs in more or less a straight line from forehead to nostrils—a Roman nose, if you will. The grizzly profile, however, is somewhat concave along this line.

If the bear rises on its hind legs or otherwise offers a good look at its front feet, claws can be a great diagnostic tool. Grizzly claws are straighter, longer, and more formidable than the black bear's, so if these instruments seem particularly prominent, you're probably looking at griz. Front-foot claw length on an adult grizzly ranges from a couple of inches (5 cm) to possibly 6 inches (15 cm); the claws are shorter on the hind feet.

Tracks can be tough to distinguish. Grizzly and black bear five-toed footprints are not inherently different, and their sizes—like the animals' weights—can overlap between the two species. Sometimes, of course, there is no doubt. No black bear track is likely to approach the 13-inch by 7-inch (33-cm x 18-cm) length and breadth of a big grizzly's hind foot (front feet are smaller). Claw marks may be the best footprint indicator. If they appear close to the toes, the tracks likely came from a black bear; if the marks seem quite distant from the toes, they probably belong to griz.

Perhaps the most important difference between the two species—from a recreationist's point of view—is personality. Grizzly expert Andy Russell said that comparing the explosiveness of grizzlies and black bears "is like standing a case of dynamite beside a sack of goose feathers." In general, grizzlies are indeed more aggressive, less predictable, and more likely to vigorously defend food or offspring than are black bears.

One theory suggests that many aspects of the grizzly's personality—and even its powerful anatomy—are, in part, evolved adaptations to an ancient, major shift in habitat preference. About two million years ago, retreating glaciers left behind vast tracts of treeless terrain teeming with food suitable for some ursine creatures. Theretofore, most bears had been forest dwellers that hid from enemies in the woods and, when necessary, escaped from danger by climbing trees. They were, in effect, fairly passive animals, because they had no need to be otherwise.

Gradually, some of these bears moved onto the newly created plains, and in the process acquired certain new attributes. With no place to hide and few trees to climb, they developed a more assertive nature—and a downright aggressive attitude concerning the protection of their young and food sources. To ward off attacks from wolves, saber-toothed cats, and other large predators, they grew bigger and stronger. Outside of the forest, they had little use for curved climbing claws; with abundant food available for the digging, straight claws became an asset. A good digger also needed extremely strong forequarters, so the prairie bear developed astounding front-end musculature. Over time, nature gradually selected for bears with these attributes, resulting in the present-day grizzly.

Oh, Give Me a Home

The female grizzly whirled and raced back across the meadow toward her pair of approaching two-year-old offspring. The young bears halted, perhaps in preparation for the reconciliation they knew had to be coming. Moments ago, the female—the cubs' lifelong protector and provider—had gruffly driven them off with strong growls and stern cuffs to the head. Perplexed, the cubs had bounded into the forest, but when their mother set off across the meadow, they followed. Now, at a run, the female rammed into the first cub, sending it reeling. The bewildered second cub dumbly accepted a bite to its shoulder before turning to escape from this mother that obviously meant business. The young pair ran off about 50 yards (46 m), then stopped to look back. The female had not moved, so the cubs began another, more timid, approach. Instantly, the female's ears lay back, her head fell below her shoulders, and she charged. This time, the cubs did not wait around. Three hundred yards (275 m) later, they looked back just in time to see their mother top the distant ridge to the west and disappear down the far side.

Grizzlies, like most wild animals, have only three requirements for survival: food, water, and a place to live. For the great bear, water is often abundant, and food is usually no problem, since a grizzly will eat almost anything. But a place to live—habitat—is another matter entirely. For every grizzly, the search for a home begins more or less the way it did for these two-year-olds, by being forced out from under mother's protective blanket to find their own niche in the world. (If there's more than one newly emancipated young grizzly, the pair [or trio] may remain together awhile—and even den together once—before going their separate ways.)

Eventually, most grizzlies settle down on a relatively well-defined chunk of land called a home range. The primary requirement of a good home range is the availability of food, and the search for those goodies is the most significant force driving grizzly location and behavior. Where food is abundant, the home range may cover only a dozen square miles (31 sq. km), but in less bountiful regions, a grizzly may forage across an area many times larger. In one Yellowstone study, male home ranges averaged more than 750 square miles (1,950 sq. km), and an Alaskan grizzly, perhaps the record holder, covered 2,200 square miles (5,720 sq. km). Generally, the home range

A grizzly's home range may encompass a variety of terrain, and its size usually is determined by how much food is available in the area. (Photo © Fred Hirschmann)

of a grizzly male will be considerably larger than that of a female, because the bigger male needs more sustenance and because a female shepherding a couple of cubs cannot travel as far.

Biologists distinguish sharply between *home range* and *territory*. Every bear—indeed, every animal—has a home range, which is nothing more than the extent of ground it covers while making a living. For neighboring grizzlies, home ranges often overlap, with two or more bears using some common terrain. Territory, on the other paw, refers to land the animal considers exclusively its own and is likely to defend against others of its kind. Grizzlies don't defend territories.

Grizzlies tend to follow the same routes through their home ranges, sometimes creating well-worn paths. (Photo © Henry H. Holdsworth)

They do, however, have unwritten mutual agreements to stay out of each other's way. Their supersensitive noses likely operate like radar to detect one another and allow graceful evasion. Another device may be tree scratching, whereby a passing bruin leaves its marks, visual and olfactory, not so much as a warning but as an announcement—a kind of home page on the grizzly Internet. Like human contracts, ursine mutual avoidance agreements are sometimes breached, but generally work well to prevent conflicts.

Grizzlies usually prefer a mix of habitat types that includes plenty of meadows and other open areas as well as forests or brushy places providing seclusion. Specifically, the boundaries where contrasting habitats meet are favorite foraging grounds for grizzlies (and a host of other species)—so much so that ecologists have coined the term *edge effect* to describe the abundance of wildlife frequenting these margin areas. Consequently, a great deal of grizzly activity occurs where forest and open land meet.

Once a grizzly establishes a home range, it develops a strong affinity for that area and, apparently, the internal navigational ability to return there if removed. It's not unusual for a grizzly to come back like a homing pigeon to its old stomping grounds after being hauled more than 100 miles (160 km) away, even across rather

Although fear of humans causes many grizzlies to spend much time in the forest, they often prefer to forage in meadows and other open areas. (Photo © Gary Schultz)

rugged terrain. This sometimes complicates the lives of wildlife managers, who try to deal with problem bears (those that learn to eat garbage, kill livestock, or otherwise hang around people) by plunking them down in a distant wilderness area. Unfortunately, "boomerang bears" risk paying for their return with their lives. Scientists aren't sure how bears implement their homing instinct; smell likely plays a role, but they may also—like certain other animals—navigate via magnetism or even the stars.

It's not difficult to identify grizzly home range when the occupant leaves tracks like these behind. (Photo © Duane Sept)

Just as grizzlies are exemplary homebodies during the winter, they become quintessential free spirits during the summer, forever wandering in search of something to eat. Instead of fully exploiting the available food in a relatively small area, the big bears tend to eat a little, then move on. Like most other backcountry travelers, grizzlies follow predictable routes and corridors—trails, ridges, shorelines, streams, and roads. In Alaska, there are ridgelines where countless generations of grizzlies have traced precisely the same steps, creating deep depressions that long ago became a permanent part of the landscape.

Undisturbed grizzlies often develop a fairly predictable daily routine. Generally, midday is a time for rest; a bear naps at a site of its own construction, often nothing more than a trampled spot in the brush or perhaps a shallow depression scraped into the ground. These spots, called day beds, are usually in timber or other cover but are often rather close to the edge of a meadow. A grizzly may establish several day beds throughout its home range and use them as needed, or simply make a new one when the sleepies hit. Grizzlies are most active at night, but they are far from purely nocturnal and may forage up to 16 hours of the day, and even that busy schedule expands as denning time approaches.

Unfortunately for grizzlies, much of their habitat long ago became human habitat, too, and in the lower 48 states, grizzlies are no longer present on 98 percent of their original range. The last state to become devoid of grizzlies was apparently Colorado. In 1967, a professional trapper confirmed the presence of a female grizzly with yearling cubs in the state's San Juan Mountains. For the next dozen years, there were no bona fide Colorado grizzly sightings, and folks assumed the bears had all vanished. Then in 1979, outfitter and bowhunter Ed Wiseman ran into a 16-year-old female grizzly near the Continental Divide in the southern part of the state, an encounter that ended when the mauled hunter killed the bear by stabbing it with a hand-held arrow. (Wiseman claimed the bear had attacked without provocation, but evidence suggested that the animal had been shot first with an arrow.) Biologists could not be sure, but some physiological signs indicated that the female had at some point produced young; if so, this meant her mate and/or offspring might still be in the region, and a cadre of grizzly searchers (official and unofficial) combed the San Juans looking for the *ghost* grizzlies. They turned up intriguing samples of grizzlyesque hair, tracks, scats, day beds, dens, and foraging activity, but no ironclad proof. Even today, optimistic grizzly supporters continue to search, but officially grizzlies are no more in Colorado. And even if a few of the big bears still hide out somewhere in the San Juans, the population almost certainly is too small to perpetuate itself for long.

Throughout much of the grizzly bear's range, people continue to appropriate grizzly habitat for their own purposes, such as homes, ski resorts, mining, logging, etc. Each new development nibbles away at the few remaining places where grizzlies exist. The thinking used to be that grizzlies require vast tracts of unbroken wilderness and that they could not tolerate humans and human activity in their domain. This theory has given way, however, to the notion that the bears can indeed survive near civilization—as long as they have access to food, water, cover, and denning areas and are not shot, harrassed, or otherwise harmed by people. The problem, it turns out, is not that grizzlies can't adapt to people, but that people won't adapt to them.

With the possible exception of the wolf, the grizzly is the most studied, talked about, loved, hated, feared, admired, controversial, political animal in North America. The grizzly has its own constituency, anti-constituency, and even its own bureaucracy. Just about everyone in the western United States, Alaska, and Canada—and many others who have never set foot in grizzlyland—has an opinion about the great bear. Although many ranchers and other denizens of grizzly habitat accept griz as a vital part of nature, plenty of folks still subscribe to the nineteenth-century credo that the only good bear is a dead bear. Of course, killing grizzlies is illegal these days (in the Lower 48, that is; they are legally hunted in Canada, Alaska, and other parts of the world), but a simple statute is not always the best deterrent out where witnesses are few and the sound of a rifle shot attracts little attention. Grizzly killers even have new watchwords: "shoot, shovel, and shut up."

Across the political canyon, ardent bear supporters, often members of one conservation group or another, scramble to protect griz from habitat loss and other threats. To them, the grizzly is one of North America's great

The battle over grizzlies is really more about land than bears. Traditional philosophy has always held that evicted bruins can go elsewhere—but we're running out of elsewheres. (Photo © Kennan Ward)

wildlife icons, an excellent indicator of the health of wild places, and the symbol of all that is natural and free. At the urging of these groups, the U.S. Fish and Wildlife Service put the grizzlies of the Lower 48 on the threatened species list in 1975, and most grizzly patrons would like to see the great bear remain under that protective umbrella. Opponents, however, point to apparent grizzly population increases—particularly in and around Yellowstone and Glacier National Parks—and say it's time to *delist* the grizzly, at least in those areas.

Caught in the political middle are the men and women—biologists, wardens, land managers, and others—charged with grizzly management. Their work can be frustrating, especially since grizzlies don't always act in their species' best interest. For example, one April day biologists found a grizzly chasing calves on a ranch near Kiowa, Montana, on the Blackfeet Indian Reservation. The biologists trapped the 400-pound (182-kg) male and shipped him 30 air miles (48 km) into the remote Bob Marshall Wilderness. But a couple of months later, the bear was back on the res-

Biologists used to think that grizzlies needed vast expanses of wilderness. Now they know the big bears can live near civilization—as long as people let them. (Photo © Henry H. Holdsworth)

ervation killing sheep. After another move and a stint of good behavior, the bear killed a cow. Again, authorities shipped him to a new area and monitored his behavior—even frightening him away from livestock with firecrackers. But when the "bad-news" bear killed yet another cow on private land, officials reluctantly ended his life with a bullet.

In a greater sense, however, the grizzly battle is not about cows and bears, but about land—and whether it should be preserved in relatively pristine condition or exploited for economic gain. Some loggers, ranchers, miners, recreationists, and others who play on or make a living from the land resent the bear—and the Endangered Species Act that sometimes ranks grizzly priorities above their own. But even as grizzlies supposedly bask in the protection of the act, subdivisions, livestock, resorts, mines, logging, and energy production gnaw away at the edges of their range. By itself, no single entrepreneurial endeavor spells doom for grizzlies, but in the aggregate, they might.

Roads are perhaps the biggest problem. They hack the land to pieces, and once the bulldozers have made their cuts, it is nearly impossible to put the "Humpty Dumpty" of habitat back together again. A road into wild

land is an entree to exploitation. If they build it, people will come—to hunt, fish, camp, watch birds, cut firewood, build homes, log, or poach wildlife—and large numbers of people usually mean trouble for grizzlies. Some of the big bears will go elsewhere (as long as there is an elsewhere), while others will stay—and perhaps get into trouble or get shot. Invariably, the local demise of the grizzly begins with a road.

Even where roads are few and people accept the presence of grizzlies, another accouterment of civilization—garbage—can make coexistence difficult. While grizzlies have no particular interest in humans, they quickly

This Yellowstone bear and its 200 or so colleagues constitute an isolated population that is cut off genetically from other grizzly populations. (Photo © Robert E. Barber)

learn that wherever there are people, there is also garbage. For several decades earlier in this century, dumps within Yellowstone National Park (and, to a lesser extent, Glacier) attracted large numbers of grizzlies (as well as black bears), which in turn attracted lots of people. Like spokes emanating from a wheel hub, bear trails led in all directions from the Yellowstone dumps. So worn were some of these paths that they were still discernible more than a decade after authorities closed the dumps around 1970.

Today, garbage in grizzly habitat—usually in the form of a household can or two—is still a problem, because it can lure bears into contact with people, where the bruins all too often become pests and pose dangers. When that happens, the bears always lose. Biologists and wildlife managers are forever preaching about proper garbage storage and disposal, but with so many people living in grizzly habitat these days, there usually is no shortage of temptations for old griz.

Another problem is poaching. Grizzlies are valuable animals, and not just to wildlife supporters who thrill to the sight of one on a distant hillside. Wealthy pseudo-sportsmen have paid up to $10,000 for the opportunity to illegally shoot a grizzly, and even the bear's component parts bring incredible prices. In China, Japan, Korea, and other nations of the Orient, folks clinging to ancient legends about bear virility and power annually pay millions of dollars for ursine gall bladders, paws, meat, blood, and bones as treatment for everything from baldness to impotence to hangovers. A grizzly gall bladder may bring $3,000 and claws $75 apiece.

Meanwhile, conservationists are looking for new grizzly habitats—or rather existing habitats that might benefit from the introduction of new grizzlies—but the options are not extensive. The San Juan Mountains area of Colorado is one possibility, but most interest these days centers on a rugged expanse of land in Idaho and Montana anchored by the Selway-Bitterroot and the Frank Church–River of No Return Wilderness areas. Grizzlies once lived there, and some experts suspect a few might still survive in these remote regions. One study suggests that the area might be suitable for 200 to 400 grizzlies, and the bureaucratic wheels have begun to turn in the direction of effecting grizzly releases there, possibly before the turn of the century. Many people, however, don't want more grizzlies around, so such a reintroduction is likely to be an uphill battle.

Crucial to long-term, Lower-48 grizzly prosperity may be a concept called habitat linkage. According to biologists, an isolated population of grizzlies (or any other species) can ensure its genetic diversity only by maintaining a relatively large number of breeders or by periodically receiving an infusion of new genes. If, on occasion, a grizzly from one population can mate within another small population, the recipient gene pool will likely remain healthy. The problem is that one of the cornerstone grizzly populations, Yellowstone's, is completely insular; that is, the area is surrounded by a moat of terrain devoid of the big bears. No new grizzlies migrate to Yellowstone, and no Yellowstone grizzlies emigrate elsewhere. The same threat would arise for the grizzly population proposed for the Selway-Bitterroot Wilderness. Grizzlies thus sequestered run the risk of having their gene pool turn stagnant and their vitality wane. (Grizzlies in the northern Rockies and Cascades are somewhat less restricted, since they border Canadian bear habitat, but within the United States, they, too, are isolated.) This is where linkage comes in. Émigré grizzlies can travel, of course, only by walking through connecting—or linking—corridors of suitable habitat. But keeping these habitat linkages available for grizzly use—that is, free of manmade impediments to bear travel—will not be easy.

The bottom line of all this is that grizzlies, if they are to maintain viable populations in the Lower 48, need to have their shrinking habitat protected, a goal more dependent upon politics than upon science.

Conclusion

With strong, even strides the grizzly climbs the cirque's talus-covered slope, leaving the little lake and treeline lying far below. The day is bright and warm. In all directions there is no sign of human presence—only mountains, valleys, forest, and sky. Finally, with a grunt of extra effort, the great bear pulls itself up to stand astride the narrow arête. On the other side, a wide glacial valley rolls toward the horizon. Here, at the top of the world, the summer wind rushes past, rippling the animal's dark, silver-tipped hair. With head erect and eyes glistening, the bear surveys its realm, an aura of bestial confidence enveloping its every move. The grizzly is, without question, lord of the mountain.

What good are grizzlies? It's a common query, but too often the answer, eminently obvious to many, comes in a language fully foreign to anyone who must ask the question. The grizzly is a symbol of the earth the way it used to be, history living on the hoof. The bear represents wilderness, freedom, unspoiled land, clean water and air, and an indomitable spirit. The grizzly is the miner's canary for vast regions; if the land has grizzlies, the rest of the fauna and flora are likely in good shape, too. Beyond that, the grizzly—even unseen—lends an ambience of wonder and enrichment to the natural world, a sense of intrigue and mystery. In his book *The Great Bear: Contemporary Writings on the Grizzly*, John Murray puts it this way: "The presence of even one grizzly on the land elevates the mountains, deepens the canyons, chills the winds, brightens the stars, darkens the forests, and quickens the pulse of all who enter it."

Predicting the future of the grizzly is not easy. They may well continue the decline that is now a century and a half old, and it is entirely possible that before today's teenagers become grandparents, the grizzly will die off in the Lower 48. A few bears might linger on for an additional decade or so, but with the gene pool drained almost dry, they would be but living anachronisms.

Or, these bears might somehow change their ways, somehow effect an 11th-hour adaptation to buy a little time or even arrest their fall. In Europe, some brown bear populations learned to survive by becoming nocturnal recluses that avoid human contact at all costs. Conceivably, the grizzlies of the contigu-

Here in Banff National Park and wherever else they exist, grizzlies—like craggy peaks and pristine forests—are symbols of all that is natural, wild, and free. (Photo © Michael H. Francis)

ous states might do likewise.

Or, they might bounce back stronger than ever. Sometimes, a declining species peeks into the abyss of extinction or extirpation and steps back. Once, wild turkeys and pronghorns were thought to be headed for history's boneyard. Today, they thrive in teeming flocks and herds. Might not the grizzlies of the Lower 48 make a similar rebound on a much smaller scale?

If the grizzly is to survive, people must evolve a new attitude, a fresh ethic. We must be willing to give up a little timber, a housing development, mine, or ski resort so we can forever keep the great bear. (Photo © Henry H. Holdsworth)

Or, grizzlies may continue clinging to the tenuous status quo.

Ticking off these options like so many menu items omits a key ingredient, however. Grizzlies are not autonomous. They do not live in a vacuum. Grizzlies exist at the pleasure of people, and the trail that eventually leads to grizzly prosperity—or demise—will carry the tracks of human, not ursine, feet. The demise of the grizzly can be forestalled. It is a matter of cost and of will. If enough resources are devoted to stopping poachers, protecting crucial habitat, and learning about the great bear, then the grizzly might roam the wilds forever. It is a choice the public must make. We have it in our power to let the grizzly of the Lower 48 live or to snuff the bear out like a candle at bedtime.

If the grizzly bear is to survive among us, there must be a shifting attitude, a fresh ethic on the Main Streets of the United States. More people must agree that we humans need not be universal masters, that we need not control every living and nonliving thing. Here and there, we must be willing to give up a little timber, a housing development, a ski resort, a hiking trail, a road, or other trappings of our civilization so that grizzlies can survive. We must learn again to coexist, as ancient peoples did, with the great bear.

Index

Above: Worldwide Range of the Grizzly Bear/Brown Bear (*Ursus arctos*)

Left: North American Grizzly Bear Range Around 1850

Present Range of the North American Grizzly Bear

North
Cascades

Selkirk

Cabinet-Yaak

Northern
Continental
Divide

Yellowstone

Range of the North American
grizzly bear

Range of the Kodiak brown bear

Grizzly Bear/Brown Bear Facts

Species: *Ursus arctos*

Subspecies: *U. a. horribilis* and *U. a. middendorffi* (in North America); many more in Eurasia.

Common Names: grizzly, brown bear, silvertip, Old Ephraim, Kodiak brown bear (*U. a. middendorffi*)

Average Weight: Male: 400 to 600 pounds (182–272 kg)

                Female: 300 to 450 pounds (136–204 kg)

Average Length: Male: 60 to 72 inches (152–183 cm)

                Female: 56 to 65 inches (142–165 cm)

Average Height: Male: 40 to 48 inches (102–122 cm)

                Female: 36 to 48 inches (91–122 cm)

Kodiak brown bears generally are larger than grizzlies. A male Kodiak may weigh 850 pounds (386 kg), stand 54 inches (137 cm) tall, and measure 96 inches (244 cm) in length.

Longevity: 15 to 20 years in the wild, possibly 25 years in captivity

Color: brown, tan, blond, or black (sometimes with silver-tipped hairs)

Top Speed: 35 mph (56 kph)

Age at Sexual Maturity: 3 ½ years, though many females are 6 or 7 (or even 8 or 9) when they give birth for the first time

Frequency of Reproduction: 1 to 3 cubs every 3 or 4 years

Size of Cubs at Birth: 10 to 20 ounces (284–567 g)

Range: Alaska, western Canada, portions of some western states. Eurasian subspecies inhabit Scandinavia, Bulgaria, and other parts of northern and eastern Europe; parts of western Europe; several former Soviet republics; and portions of China and other Asian nations.